# Infinite Empowerment

## Unlock Your Power & Infinite Success
## Workbook Journal

Amy R. Woods

Infinite Empowerment: Unlock Your Power & Infinite Success Workbook Journal is a work of my own creation.

The information in this book was correct at the time of publication, and the Author does not assume any liability for loss or damage caused by errors or omissions, again, this is my perspective, opinion, and experience, so it has been written as such.

ISBN - 978-1-961185-03-6

www.inomniaparatuspublishing.com

# I Dedicate This To...

This workbook is dedicated to my business coach Elysia Skye, my publisher Megs Thompson, my husband & The Sapphire Collective Group of women for their unrelenting support, encouragement, inspiration & dedication to creating a better world to live in.

To my clients who are amazing female entrepreneurs, coaches & course creators who've climbed huge mountains, overcome larger than life circumstances & come back even stronger. Ready to empower their mind & define life on their terms.

You are my purpose & the reason I always strive to leap further up than where I am.

# Empowerment is a choice.

Choice is what creates all opportunity and allows the impossible to become possible.

Believing in your decisions, your choices, and listening to your intuition is key in making the choices that will allow abundance in your life.

Throughout this workbook you will find prompts for journaling. Use this workbook to open your mind to where you are at right now in this moment, to see where you want to go, and to map out how to get there.

Choose to take action and plan those actionable steps so you know what to expect along the way.

Choose to grow and journal on what to expect.

Knowing, choice, action, and absolute belief is your power.

No one can ever take that from your soul.

"You Are One
With All The
Abundance
Of The Universe"

~Amy R. Woods

# Set An Intention

Set an intention for what you want to occur with this workbook. What results are you wanting to receive from doing the work inside of this book? Allow yourself to seek out what it is you are wanting and needing.

_____
_____
_____
_____
_____
_____
_____
_____
_____
_____
_____
_____
_____
_____
_____
_____
_____

To begin list out what you are great at. What are your natural talents? What have you accomplished? What are you skilled at? Doing so allows you to receive a knowing about how powerful you truly are. Follow the prompts below to keep you organized.

Natural Talents:

_____

_____

_____

_____

_____

_____

_____

_____

_____

_____

_____

_____

_____

_____

_____

_____

_____

_____

_____

# What Have You Accomplished:

_____

_____

_____

_____

_____

_____

_____

_____

_____

_____

_____

_____

_____

_____

_____

_____

_____

_____

_____

_____

_____

_____

_____

_____

_____

_____

_____

_____

_____

# What are you skilled at:

_____
_____
_____
_____
_____
_____
_____
_____
_____
_____
_____
_____
_____
_____
_____
_____
_____
_____
_____
_____
_____
_____
_____
_____
_____
_____
_____

How do you feel when you are complimented on the items above?

_____
_____
_____
_____
_____
_____
_____
_____
_____
_____
_____
_____
_____
_____
_____
_____
_____
_____
_____
_____
_____
_____
_____
_____
_____
_____
_____
_____
_____

Part of empowering your mind is about being really honest about yourself, your life, what you wish would change, and how you want to feel. Follow the prompts below and write out in detail the answers. Remember no one else will see this, you are safe, and this is about reflection. This can be good reflections and wanted changes. There is no wrong answer.

List out everything either in your life, in your business, in your relationships that you love.

_____
_____
_____
_____
_____
_____
_____
_____
_____
_____
_____
_____
_____
_____

List out the changes you want to see happen in your life, your business, your relationships, etc..

_____
_____
_____
_____
_____
_____
_____
_____
_____
_____
_____
_____
_____
_____
_____
_____
_____
_____
_____
_____
_____
_____
_____
_____
_____
_____
_____
_____
_____

In the order that you can start to accomplish those changes write out the HOW you will start to do so. The ones that you will need more resources for list last. We will tackle resources next.

_____
_____
_____
_____
_____
_____
_____
_____
_____
_____
_____
_____
_____
_____
_____
_____
_____
_____
_____
_____
_____
_____
_____
_____
_____
_____
_____
_____

Resources you will need to accomplish your goals. List out the specific resources you will need to accomplish your goals. For example; money, professional collaborations, mentors, programs, etc... How will you accomplish receiving those resources? Do not worry if it feels unattainable. This will work out as you open opportunity. The point of this exercise is to know the path to what it is you are wanting to accomplish.

_____
_____
_____
_____
_____
_____
_____
_____
_____
_____
_____
_____
_____
_____
_____
_____
_____
_____
_____
_____
_____
_____

*It Doesn't Matter
Who You Are,
Where You Come From,
The Ability To Triumph
Begins With You
Always*

~ Oprah

# Mindset:

Empowerment is a state of being. It's knowing you can choose to do what it is you are wanting to do without fear or doubt, without knowing how things will turn out, while trusting yourself and listening to your intuition. Again this section will be about being honest with yourself, knowing you are safe, and this is a judgment free zone. If you feel yourself starting to judge your own answers use the notes area in the back of this workbook to express that judgment and the feelings or situations surrounding that judgment.

This section will be about letting go of the past, accepting responsibility, and moving your life forward. To do so there is a process and I want you to allow it to be easy by not judging yourself or the past.

*What circumstance is in need of forgiveness?*
*Who is involved? What has it made you feel like?*

_____
_____
_____
_____
_____
_____
_____
_____
_____
_____
_____
_____
_____
_____
_____
_____
_____
_____
_____
_____
_____

Forgiveness is never about the other people involved. This is about you releasing the energy you have attached to the situation and circumstance. The people involved are human, imperfect, and while what happened should require an apology, most won't admit if they were wrong.

By releasing YOUR energy from the situation you will be ok with someone being apologetic or not, because it won't be of importance to you any longer.

To do this sit in a quiet room or area, close your eyes, start taking deep breaths in and out fully until you are relaxed. Visualize this situation and the people in it with each of you holding onto a chord attached to each other, the scenes in the situation, and what you hold of importance.

Cut your chord from them and pull it back to you and visualize them pullingn their chord back to them. This represents you npulling your energy back to you. Its ok if you become emotional that is release. Allow it to flow and allow it to happen. Receive your own energy back.

How are you feeling? Take a break if you need to this part can be quite emotional. Journal below about your experience with it.

_____
_____
_____
_____
_____
_____
_____
_____
_____
_____
_____
_____
_____
_____
_____
_____
_____
_____
_____
_____
_____
_____
_____
_____
_____
_____
_____

What are you avoiding? Part of choice and changing how we live is taking responsibility for what we avoid. When we take responsibility we empower our choices even more. My mentor told me there is treasure in what we avoid and she is right. Discover what you are avoiding and the steps you can take to stop doing so.

_____
_____
_____
_____
_____
_____
_____
_____
_____
_____
_____
_____
_____
_____
_____
_____
_____
_____
_____
_____
_____
_____
_____

You Can,
You Should,
and If You Are
Brave Enough
To Start,
You Will.
~ Stephen King

Now let's make choices and empower where you want to go. The following pages will be about your ideas, your wants, your desires and mapping how to get there. Go all the way to the end to create your action plan. It will be your choice to take action on it. Of course if you want even more support you can always go to www.infinitysalessystems.com/program and choose to invest in creating the life you want.

*Let's have some fun!*

# 1. Want or desire

# 2. What do you need to reach your want or desire?

3. How will you feel when you reach that want or desire?

4. What do you need to do first to start implementing your actionable steps to reach that goal?

_____
_____
_____
_____
_____
_____
_____
_____
_____
_____
_____
_____
_____
_____
_____
_____
_____
_____
_____
_____
_____
_____
_____
_____
_____
_____

5. When will you start taking action and when will that action be finished?

_____

_____

_____

_____

_____

_____

_____

_____

_____

_____

_____

_____

_____

_____

_____

_____

_____

_____

_____

_____

_____

_____

Empowerment is all about choosing. Making one choice and moving on it. Once a choice/decision is made what will you choose everyday to do so you stay committed until it is done. What about when it gets hard because it will and life is still going to be life. The rest of this book is your journal to do as you wish. Use these prompts to keep creating your own.

## Suggestions to journal on:

Accountability~ How will you keep yourself accountable? Do you need help or a mentor to help you do so?

Money Map: Map out what money you will require and how you will choose to raise that capitol. There is no wrong answer here and its never impossible.

Always track your mindset and how you are feeling as you move through your processes. Feel them fully and then journal on HOW you want to feel. Eliminate the fear by bringing a neutral space to the fear.

How can you ask for support. Communicating to loved ones is so important and necessary to your success. If you do not have that support you may have to hire it and start surrounding yourself with people who do. No one becomes a success alone.

Enjoy the rest of the journal and inspiration through out these pages. If you are interested in being able to work further with me please go to [www.infinitysalessystems.com/program](www.infinitysalessystems.com/program) for more information. I've also included some details about my own personal story sprinkled throughout the following notes pages.

You were put on this earth to achieve your greatest self, to live out your purpose, and to do it courageously.

~ Steve Maraboli

When I was homeless I saw how my 'everyday life' had become a normal everyday life to many others.

I had the choice to allow this life to become my normal, to wait the two years for help, to choose to do something about it myself, to take radical responsibility for where I was at in my life, and to take radical action to change how my life was being lived.

*I chose to take responsibility and to take radical action.*

This created fast movement and I was no longer homeless within 2 months time.

It's always about choice.

~Amy R. Woods

After waking up in the hospital from my husband finding me with a gun in my mouth, I realized I had a choice.

I could get busy dying or get busy living.

## I chose to live.

I chose to start college a week later.

I chose to start a business two years later.

I chose me & 4 years later I'm a successful happy business owner.

Choose YOU.

That is empowerment.

~Amy R. Woods

# Infinity is defined as forever.

To keep going.

Unboundedness.

Everlasting.

Legacy.

No ending.

To Love Is Infinite.

Infinity Sales Systems is about more than sales.
It's about everlasting empowerment,
unbounded living, leaving a legacy, and love.

www.infinitysalessystems.com/program